Ten P
about R

ex libris

Candlestick Press

Published by:

Candlestick Press,
Diversity House, 72 Nottingham Road, Arnold, Nottingham NG5 6LF
www.candlestickpress.co.uk

Design and typesetting by Craig Twigg

Printed by Ratcliff & Roper Print Group, Nottinghamshire, UK

Selection and Introduction © Stephen Keeler, 2022

Cover illustration © Hannah Forward, 2022
www.hannahforward.com

Candlestick Press monogram © Barbara Shaw, 2008

© Candlestick Press, 2022

ISBN 978 1 913627 16 4

Acknowledgements

The poems in this pamphlet are reprinted from the following books, all by
permission of the publishers listed unless stated otherwise. Every effort has been
made to trace the copyright holders of the poems published in this book. The
editor and publisher apologise if any material has been included without
permission or without the appropriate acknowledgement, and would be glad to be
told of anyone who has not been consulted.

Thanks are due to all the copyright holders cited below for their kind permission:

Helen Allison, *The Result is What You See Today: Poems About Running* (Smith/
Doorstop, 2019). Carole Bromley, *The Result is What You See Today: Poems
About Running* (Smith/Doorstop, 2019). Wanda Coleman, *Hand Dance* (Black
Sparrow Press, 1993) by permission of David R. Godine. Mark Granier, *Fade
Street* (Salt, 2010) by kind permission of the author. Stephen Keeler, poem first
published in this pamphlet. Jenny King, *The Result is What You See Today: Poems
About Running* (Smith/Doorstop, 2019). Glyn Maxwell, *Boys at Twilight: Poems
1990-1995* (Bloodaxe Books, 2000) www.bloodaxebooks.com. Eugene Ethelbert
Miller, *First Light: New & Selected Poems* (Black Classic Press, 1994). Mandy
Sutter, *The Result is What You See Today: Poems About Running* (Smith/
Doorstop, 2019). David Wagoner, *Traveling Light: Collected & New Poems*
(University of Illinois Press, 1999).

All permissions cleared courtesy of Suzanne Fairless-Aitken
c/o Swift Permissions swiftpermissions@gmail.com

Where poets are no longer living, their dates are given.

Introduction

There is a literally painful irony in a runner-poet sitting at his desk, as I am now, selecting poems about running while nursing a bad, frustrating and possibly long-term knee injury preventing me from even light jogging.

Frailty and strength; anxiety and determination; fear and perseverance – these are what we write about when we write about running. These, too, are what we write about when we write about the human condition. When running becomes a metaphor for life itself, it should not surprise us to be moved by Mandy Sutter's portrait of her father, the old trail runner, or by the realities of age running against time, in Mark Granier's 'Stopwatch'.

We runners talk in careless 'k's – a five, an eight, a ten. But Helen Allison's highland forest, Wanda Coleman's "brilliant fruitless flight" and Eugene Miller losing count of the miles remind us of the intimacies which make every run different and intensely personal. Theirs are poems, too, which deftly evoke the interplay between heightened alertness and dreamlike abstraction which long-distance runners especially will recognise at once.

Sweat-soaked, tech-embellished and intense, running has become a democratic urban pastime just as it remains an elite professional sport. Jenny King's urban runners are perhaps too easy a target but even they suggest the geographical consciousness which David Wagoner celebrates, breathless, as well as that hint of existential solitude which might be something more than just the intrinsic loneliness of the long-distance runner. For anyone looking for an excuse *not* to Just Do It, Carole Bromley offers a dozen pretty convincing reasons which runners of every degree of commitment will recognise.

Read, enjoy and ponder – but make sure you go before it starts raining or it gets dark or the dog-walkers come out or ... because as Glyn Maxwell asserts, "It did me good. I hope it does you gooder."

Stephen Keeler

Twelve Reasons Why Not

Dogs
Lorry drivers whistling
Neighbours making remarks
Rain
Self-consciousness
Your belly
Making the time
Your laughable progress
Stage fright
Hitting the wall
The last half mile
Being overtaken by the pantomime camel

Carole Bromley

Marathon

it's a strange time which finds me jogging
in early morning
the deadness of sleep alive in this world
the empty parks filled with unloved strangers
buildings grey with solitude
now near the end of another decade
i am witness to the loss of my twenties
a promise invisible
i run without purpose
far from the north star
i run with the sound of barking dogs closing in
i have lost count of the miles
i am older and nothing much matters
or has changed

Eugene Ethelbert Miller

Running

Running across country easily at evening, taking the stones
As easily as stubble, running from nothing but going
Past fences swamped by berries, into a high field
And down a long furrow sloping into wheat, then climbing
To scatter the booming pheasants, crossing and turning
Where cinders slant to a bridge, then underneath
And down a green creekbank over the crowns of logs
Through shallow water and ferns, stumbling into the woods
To a clearing gold as a haystack, faltering
Now, breath going back, and forth, catching
And breaking, then running down to the ground
Into a deeper grassbank, sprawling, raking the air
And sweating it out, a stretch of sky thrown backward,
Blinking, scraping at breath
As brokenly as heart-beats, everything in the rib-cage running
And running, going ahead
Without me across country, the deep breath burning.

David Wagoner (1926 – 2021)

Runners in Town

Runners slip through the crowd, nip
round shopping-heavy pushchairs, on
past gossiping groups and are gone
into a sort of fourth dimension.

Hardly present, they slide
between minute and minute, intent
on escaping what time once meant,
while shoppers stare, asking each other

Was that Paul? Was that Sue? unsure
whether the flickering figures half seen
from behind might have been
the friends they knew, or thought they knew.

Jenny King

Nocturne

running in place
my tongue has grown strong and hard
my pace is steadier my step surer
measured as circles move around me and define
this frayed self the center of at least one stubborn
cosmos
here i sweat the days
humming because rhythm makes persistence possible
occasionally breaking into song-and-dance
aware of the weight that impedes momentum
aware of wind factor and traction
(to wish i were dead? easy. the one wish that
always comes true)
as the hum of unseen fellow runners
urges me on thru this brilliant fruitless flight
point of departure is a certainty
arrival a myth
as i streak along the beginning turning back on
itself again and again. my focus dead ahead
peering. to see if
this is the dark that precedes dawn
or the darkness before the dark

Wanda Coleman (1946 – 2013)

Mr F Gets Fit
Homage to the Presiding Spirit of Amherst

I jogged away from town on a dim day
That didn't know me, though I knew my way,
Or thought as much. The way seemed unimpressed
And thought it ought to put me to some test,

For not one path I confidently chose
But steepened. If I slackened then they rose,
And took my breath as if they needed air
For mischief and had singled out my share.

Like I was someone that today could spare.
Make light of, brush away, not its affair.
One that today could do its work without,
Be fond of, being unconcerned about.

On these new ways by which I had to pass
Came none with any notion who I was,
But all, by light too brief for friendship found,
Suggested I begin by turning round,

So I should face where I belonged: elsewhere.
But I had run too much from here to there
Not to prefer to walk from there to here,
As I began to do, not to appear

Unneighborly to neighbors. And it took
Ten times as long, by any watchman's book
And no less upward than it was before.
As if the toll is always to be more

To gain admittance at a snow-white gate,
And tread the stony path in no fit state
For any sight but mine. So I doubt if I
Shall jog again this side of a white sky.

But I may get intolerably heated
Should you so much as mutter that I cheated.
I woulda jogged forever if I coulda.
It did me good. I hope it does you gooder.

Glyn Maxwell

Stopwatch

Over fifty now, one of those joggers who pass,
heads down – hard shins and soft knees – eyes on the grass,

I crank myself into old age, hold to the thin
muddied track made by runners, that keeps grass down.

Here I come, round and around, the tip of a second-hand
on a blank green clock, marking what will unwind

lap by lap, the lagging flesh on its beat
from what will escape it: spirited, hard-soled, fleet.

Mark Granier

Old Trail Runner

In winter, my father sets up base camp
in the one-man kitchen of his first floor flat,
hunkering by the radio, barely moving,
warmed by Calor gas and the thought
of cupboards crammed with canned
corned beef. Everything's to hand:
kettle, screwdriver, five pairs of specs.

At night, with stubborn care, he makes
the hard ascent, following the chimney up.
The view is stunning. To spite the doctor
he forgets his tablets and, fortified
by sherry and bananas, wearing a woolly hat,
bivvies on the bed-ledge; wakes
to ice on the inside of the window.

He believes in north and south, in pass
or fail. He doesn't want a Sherpa,
has no fear of heights or falling boulders;
looks up to the wolf moon. He's acclimatizing
for his next summit, the one he'll run
solo, following his long-lost brother's
route to the ridge, and on, and up.

Mandy Sutter

Cross Country

They made us run the way they tried to make
us pray as though their history passed on

were indisputable they handed down
those sentences of life-terms when we ran

we ran in black and white like northern films
our plimsolls Empire Made our singlets sized

for hopeless drooping men our cotton shorts
unseemly on the streets where mere youth

became indecent colour fading up
like joy and early Beatles' lyrics on

a Sunday afternoon the closer through
the trees we got to where the girls' school was

we'd seen those other films and ran we thought
like spies there was arousal in the air

the drooping men their broken women pale
as unformed thought their bicycles in ranks

inside the factory gates like animals
subdued in pens and when we ran we ran

goodbye to that we ran headlong footlong
on easy limbs across the unsown fields

and scrambled over stiles and through sweet trees
as blind to what it was we ran towards

as those who'd sent us out to run to walk
to smoke a roll-up meet a girl go home

chose not to contemplate the reasons why
they'd made us pray or sent us out to run.

Stephen Keeler

Culbin Forest 5K

for Julie Lawson

Our faces cold water splashed and just out of bed,
I am luminous yellow, you are fleece-lined in purple.
The birch trees stretch loose-limbed into morning,
our breathy chat startling the birds, but leaving
the pond ice intact, our rise and descent gravelled
and pine-scented, the shifting sands solid under our feet.
We waste nothing here, not word or minute, the path
to the sea always ahead, a dip saved for the next life.

Helen Allison

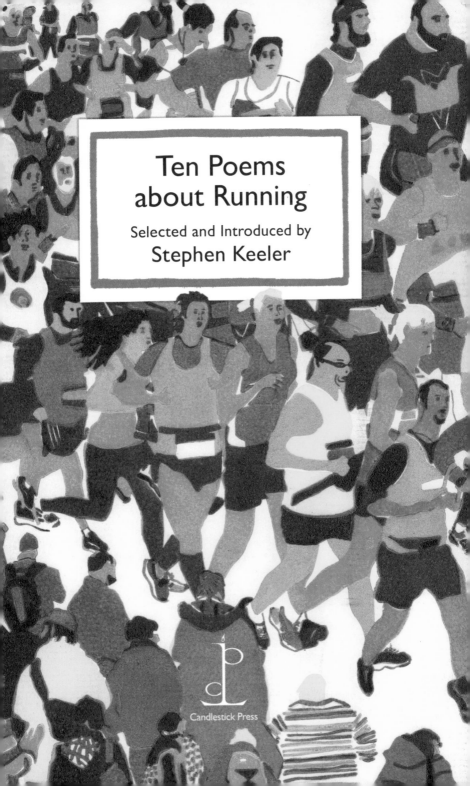

Ten Poems
about Running

Selected and Introduced by
Stephen Keeler

Candlestick Press